BEAR LIBRARY
101 GOVERNOR'S PLACE
BEAR DE   19701

04/12/1999

P9-DMK-525

ALEX
RODRIGUEZ

ALEX RODRIGUEZ

SLUGGING SHORTSTOP

Stew Thornley

Lerner Publications Company • Minneapolis

Library binding by Lerner Publications Company
Soft cover by First Avenue Editions
241 First Avenue North, Minneapolis, Minnesota 55401

Copyright © 1998 by Stew Thornley

All rights reserved. International copyright secured. No part of this book may be
reproduced or transmitted in any form or by any means, electronic or mechanical,
including photocopying and recording, or by any information storage or retrieval
system, without permission in writing from Lerner Publications Company, except for
the inclusion of brief quotations in an acknowledged review.

Website address: www.lernerbooks.com

Library of Congress Cataloging-in-Publication Data

Thornley, Stew.
    Alex Rodriguez : slugging shortstop / Stew Thornley.
       p.   cm.
    Includes bibliographical references and index.
    Summary: Presents a biography of the Seattle Mariners' shortstop, a promising
new star in baseball.
    ISBN 0–8225–3663–3 (alk. paper). — ISBN 0–8225–9825–6 (pbk. : alk. paper)
    1. Rodriguez, Alex, 1975–   —Juvenile literature. 2. Baseball players—United
States—Biography—Juvenile literature. 3. Seattle Mariners (Baseball team)—
Juvenile literature. [1. Rodriguez, Alex, 1975–   . 2. Baseball players.
3. Dominican Americans—Biography.] I. Title.
GV865.R62T56   1998
796.357'092—dc21
    [B]   98–5948

Manufactured in the United States of America
1 2 3 4 5 6 – JR – 03 02 01 00 99 98

Contents

1

Crowd Pleaser

On a warm summer day in June 1997, the Seattle Mariners began a game against the Tigers in Detroit. In the first inning, Alex Rodriguez, the Seattle Mariners' great young shortstop, drove a Felipe Lira pitch over the fence in right-center field for his ninth home run of the season. Then in the fourth inning, with the score at 5–0, Alex stepped into the batter's box and lined a single to right field, his second hit of the game.

The Tigers managed to get Alex out in the sixth inning, but they didn't have as much luck with him in the eighth. Alex hit a long drive to center field over the outstretched glove of Detroit's Brian Hunter. As the ball rattled around in the deepest part of Tiger Stadium, Alex raced around the bases, ending up at third with a triple. That made the score 10–3 in favor of Seattle. The Mariners scored four more runs in the eighth, and there was little doubt as to who would win the game.

The only suspense remaining was whether Alex could get a double, which would give him the cycle. Hitting for the cycle means getting a single, double, triple, and home run in the same game. During this particular game, a promotion was being held in which a lucky fan would win $1 million if a Seattle player hit for the cycle. The company putting up the money was confident no one would win it. It wasn't that the Mariner lineup didn't contain a lot of batters capable of getting hits of all kinds. Edgar Martinez and Jay Buhner were among the team's heavy hitters. Martinez and Buhner often got upstaged by a pair of spectacular Mariners—Alex Rodriguez and Ken Griffey Jr. Even with a lineup like this, though, hitting for the cycle is extremely rare. In the 20-year history of the Mariners, only one player had ever done it before.

In the ninth inning, Alex had his chance. He reached out and hit a looper down the right-field line. The ball dropped, barely in fair territory. As Alex neared first, Sam Mejais, the first-base coach, waved him on and shouted, "Go, go, go." From the dugout, Alex's teammates were also screaming at him to try for second. "I was going to go out and push him if I had to," Jay Buhner said later. Buhner was the only other Mariner to ever have hit for the cycle.

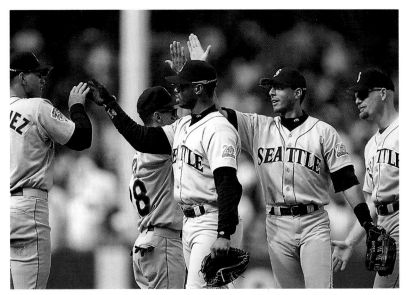

Alex (far left) exchanges high-fives with Ken Griffey Jr.
and his other teammates.

But Alex didn't need coaxing. He had his sights on
second base. Alex cruised into second base for a double. When he got there, Alex pumped his fist in the
air. Alex had completed his cycle and had made a
woman back in the state of Washington $1 million
dollars richer. "I can't wait to get home and get my
cut," he joked.

Making fans happy is nothing new to Alex. Even
though he was only 21 years old, he was playing in his
fourth season in the major leagues. Seattle fans are
used to young stars. A few years earlier the city had em-
braced Ken Griffey Jr., who broke in at the age of 19.

Alex cruises to first base after connecting with the ball.

Griffey quickly established himself as one of the top players in baseball, and Alex was following that same path—at an even faster pace.

Alex is actually part of a bumper crop of good young shortstops who have emerged in the 1990s. As some older players who had starred at shortstop retired or shifted positions, a number of new shortstops were taking their places.

Alex Rodriguez was at the head of that class.

With confidence and style, Alex has become a key member of the Mariner team.

Alex's role model and biggest fan has always been his mom, Lourdes Navarro.

A Baseball Background

Alex Rodriguez was born in New York City in 1975, but he has little recollection of the time he spent there. He doesn't even remember handling his first baseball, which he was given when he was two years old. His earliest memories go back to when he was five, and by that time he was living in the Dominican Republic, from where his parents had originally come.

The Dominican Republic takes up over half the island of Hispaniola. Haiti is on the western end of the island, which lies between the Atlantic Ocean and the Caribbean Sea. The Dominican Republic is known for sugar cane and sunny beaches. It is also known for baseball. Many stars in the major leagues in the United States came from the Dominican Republic. This includes Juan Marichal, one of the top pitchers in baseball in the 1960s and now a member of the

Hall of Fame, as well as excellent hitters like Rico Carty, Pedro Guerrero, and the Alou brothers—Felipe, Matty, and Jesus. In more recent years, the country has become famous for producing fine shortstops, such as Tony Fernandez.

As Alex got older, he began learning about some of the major league stars who had come from his country. He was most familiar, though, with someone whose career had never extended to the United States mainland. Alex's father, Victor, had once been a catcher in a Dominican professional league.

With his father by his side, Alex began learning the game of baseball. The family remained in the Dominican for only four years, however. When Alex was eight, his mother and father—along with Alex's older brother, Joe, and older sister, Susy—moved back to the United States and settled in southern Florida, outside Miami. The family didn't stay together long. After a year, Victor left the family. Alex has had little contact with his father ever since.

Victor did get his son started on baseball, and Alex says, "I always wanted to be like my dad, but my mom is my role model." His mother, Lourdes Navarro, didn't have an easy time of raising three children on her own, but she did a good job of it. Navarro would come home from one of her jobs, as a waitress, and have Alex work on his math skills by counting her tips.

Navarro encouraged Alex's interest in baseball and remembers how he could rattle off the names and statistics of players in the major leagues. "He was very focused from the time he was a child and just wasn't interested in anything else," she said. But his mother made sure Alex understood there was more to life than baseball. "I don't care if you turn out to be a terrible ballplayer. I just want you to be a good person," she said.

The players Alex chose as his baseball idols were great people as well as great stars. He kept a poster of Cal Ripken Jr., the Baltimore Orioles' outstanding shortstop, over his bed. His other heroes were Dale Murphy of the Atlanta Braves and Alan Trammell of the Detroit Tigers. Murphy and Trammell both wore number 3. Because of that, Alex chose 3 as his uniform number.

Cal Ripken Jr.

Alex marveled at how much better the baseball conditions were in the United States than in the Dominican Republic. "In the Dominican Republic, playing ball was tougher. No one had anything. In the U. S., there were $200 gloves, and the fields were like paradise," Alex recalled.

The game was still the same, though. He played constantly with his older brother. "He pitched to me in our games, and he always let me win—until the end of the game. Then he'd go on and beat me," Alex said. "It made me want to get better. I'd cry when I'd lose. Then I'd cry when we stopped playing."

Playing against older boys was something Alex got used to. He was too good to stay among players of his own age, so he was often moved up to higher leagues. "I was mad about it," Alex said, "because I could never dominate."

Alex watched a lot of television as he grew up, but he still made sure he was doing something worthwhile. The family had cable television, which meant Alex could watch baseball games from all over the country. So he did. He studied the hitters. He paid attention to what pitches they liked and where they hit the ball.

Alex was fortunate to have known some men who looked out for him after his father left the family. One was Eddie Rodriguez, who ran a Boys Club in Miami. Alex spent a great deal of time at the Boys Club.

Another role model for Alex was J. D. Arteaga Sr., the father of his best friend. Arteaga knew Alex was destined for greatness and told his son to keep an eye on his friend. "One day, my dad told me Alex was the best player he'd ever seen," recalls J. D. Arteaga Jr. "He [Alex] was 11 years old. I thought, 'Crazy man, how can you say that?' But now look. I guess my dad was a pretty good scout."

In addition to being a good scout, Arteaga Sr. was a good father—to both his own son and to Alex. "He was the father I didn't have," says Alex. "Everything he gave to his son, he gave to me."

Arteaga Sr. took the boys to games, he bought them baseball gloves and equipment, and he watched over them, no matter what they were doing or what sport they were playing. It was while watching J. D. Jr. and Alex play football, when the boys were in tenth grade, that Arteaga suffered a heart attack and died.

Alex felt the loss of the man who had taken him under his wing as much as Arteaga's own son. But he also thought it was fitting that the heart attack happened at a sporting event and that Arteaga must have died happy. "That was the perfect way for him to go," says Alex, "watching us play."

Soon after Arteaga passed away, Alex made a commitment to his future. He knew he had special talents, in sports and in other areas of life, and was determined to do all that he could with them.

Alex was an All-Conference quarterback for the
Westminster Warriors in 1991.

3
Stretching for Stardom

The Rodriguez family wasn't rich, but Lourdes Navarro worked hard to make sure her children got a good education. She worked at two jobs to earn enough money to send her youngest son, Alex, to Westminster Christian, a private high school with about 300 students.

As a sophomore, Alex played three sports for the Westminster Warriors. He was a point guard on the basketball team until his mother limited his activities to two sports so he could spend more time on his studies. He played quarterback on the football team until he decided to give up football and concentrate on the sport he most loved—baseball. "It was as if I had baseball in my blood," Alex said.

Rich Hofman was the baseball coach at Westminster, as he had been since starting the program in the late 1970s. He knew he had a special player in Alex and called the opportunity to coach him, "a once-in-a-lifetime experience."

Alex improved greatly from year to year on the Warrior baseball team. After an outstanding season as a sophomore in 1991, he began to have an inkling of how good he was and how far he could go. "Scouts told me if I kept it up, I had a good chance to be a good player and a high draft pick," Alex said. He started thinking about what he would do when his high school years were over. He could go to college and play baseball there; but if a major league team drafted him, he would have the opportunity to go straight into professional baseball. Each year in June, major league baseball teams draft players who have graduated from high school or who play college ball. Teams take turns choosing players and then offer contracts to those they pick.

But the decision to play in college or in the pros was one he didn't have to face right away. For the time being, he could continue concentrating on playing. He was great again in 1992 and helped Westminster finish the season as the top-ranked high school team in the entire country, with a record of 33 wins and 2 losses. The Warriors were named national champions by *Baseball America* and the National High School Baseball Coaches Association.

Alex wasn't done playing baseball for the year. After the high school season, he joined a United States team.

The Westminster baseball team had an outstanding season in 1992. In this team picture, Coach Hofman is in the top row, far left. Alex is in the top row, fourth from the right.

The team, made up of 17- and 18-year-olds, competed in the World Junior Championships in Monterrey, Mexico, in August 1992. Alex tied with teammate Jerrod Wong for most home runs and led the U. S. squad with 16 **runs batted in (RBIs)** in 13 games. Having the chance to play with and against players from around the country and around the world was a new and exciting challenge.

Alex began receiving even more attention from pro scouts. If these scouts were having trouble keeping track of all the fine talent that had been coming out of southern Florida, it was understandable. There had been many great players from this area. Many of them were Latinos. And not only that, several of them were named Alex.

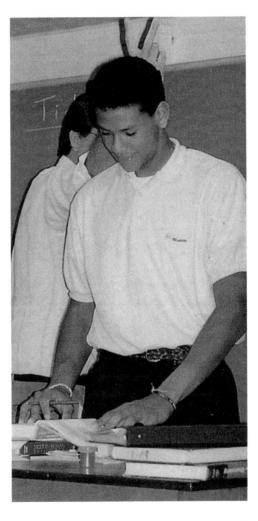

In high school, Alex stood out at school as an excellent student as well as a great athlete.

Alex Rodriguez lived only a few minutes from his friend, Alex Gonzalez, who played shortstop for the nearby Killian High School baseball team. Gonzalez graduated in 1991, the same year as another standout player, Alex Ochoa of Hialeah-Miami Lakes. If that wasn't enough, Alex Fernandez had been a great pitcher for Pace High School in Miami before graduating in 1988. Two years later, Fernandez reached the majors with the Chicago White Sox.

Even though the name game made things confusing, scouts had no trouble predicting stardom for Alex Rodriguez. Many thought he would be the first player selected in the draft after his senior season in 1993. Being marked for such greatness can put a lot of pressure on a young man. Alex dealt with it by learning from another ball player who had been through the same thing.

Derek Jeter and Alex first met over the phone. They were introduced to one another by a mutual friend. Jeter had been the first high school player taken in the 1992 draft and was playing his first season of pro ball in the New York Yankees' organization. The following spring, the two met in person. Jeter was in southern Florida for spring training and took the opportunity to see a college ball game at the University of Miami, a school that was recruiting Alex.

Alex wasn't sure if he would play college ball or go straight into the pros. There was a lot to sort out, and Jeter did what he could to help Alex. "We've been great friends ever since," Alex says.

Around this same time, Alex went to the Baltimore Orioles spring training camp in Fort Lauderdale.

Manager John Oates introduced him to Cal Ripken. "Every time I looked up the rest of that spring, I saw Alex," Oates said.

The Westminster Warriors had new baseball facilities in the spring of 1993. Two months after the team had won the national championship the year before, Hurricane Andrew swept through. Along its path of destruction, it hit the Warriors' field. Luckily for the Warriors, a local contractor donated his services toward rebuilding the facility. Westminster ended up with new fences, dugouts, and bleachers.

Those bleachers were usually full in 1993, thanks to the many people who came out to watch Alex play. Many of those were baseball scouts, armed with stopwatches and radar guns. The watches clicked on and off every time Alex ran the bases, giving the impression of crickets in the stands. The radar guns recorded the speed of pitches that Alex had to hit. The scouts noticed something strange whenever Alex came to bat. Their radar guns showed pitchers routinely throwing five miles per hour faster when facing Alex. Great players can bring out the best in others. Alex was able to do this with pitchers, who rose to the challenge of facing a great hitter.

"You can't imagine the pressure he has had to go through," said Coach Hofman. "We had big crowds everywhere just to see him play. And every pitcher pitched to him like it was the last out of the World

Series. I've never seen a player command so much attention, yet he's handled it with a great deal of humility. There's been a crush of agents and scouts everywhere we've gone this year and it's been tough on him."

Alex makes a play at shortstop.

Alex led his team through another strong season during his senior year at Westminster.

Alex dealt with the pressure and put on quite a show for the scouts. Through the first 10 games, Alex had a **batting average** of .606.

The Seattle Mariners would have the top pick in the 1993 draft and had a scout at every one of Westminster's games. Other teams, whose draft picks were so far down that they would have no chance to select Alex, still had scouts present. "We just appreciate seeing a good ballplayer," they'd tell Coach Hofman.

Of course, the pro teams would be competing with more than each other for Alex. Although he was interested in getting to the majors as soon as possible, Alex had also accepted a **scholarship** to play baseball at the University of Miami. Eventually he would have to choose between college and the pros. But first, he had a season to complete.

Alex hoped to help the Warriors win a national championship for the second straight year in 1993.

Unfortunately, the team failed to make it even to the state playoffs, losing a qualifying game. Alex committed a pair of costly **errors** in the game. Even with the disappointing ending, Westminster had finished the season with a record of 28–5. Alex had finished the year with a .505 batting average, along with 9 home runs and 36 RBIs. He also stole 35 bases without being thrown out even once.

Alex was a finalist for the Golden Spikes Award, which is presented to the top amateur player in the country, including college players. Alex was only the second high school player ever to be a finalist for the award. Ken Griffey Jr. had been the first, in 1987.

The Golden Spikes Award went to Darren Dreifort, a hard-throwing pitcher at Wichita State University. However, Alex was honored as the USA Baseball Junior Player of the Year and Gatorade's National Student Athlete in baseball. Those awards meant a great deal to Alex because both had been won the year before by his friend, Derek Jeter.

In his three seasons on the Westminster baseball team, Alex had hit .419 with 17 home runs, 70 runs batted in, and 90 stolen bases. The Warriors had won 86, lost 13, and tied 1 game in the years that Alex played for them.

Alex had done practically everything that could be done at this level. The question now was what the next level would be—college or the pros?

After graduating from high school, Alex wasn't sure where he would be playing baseball next.

4
Moving Up

The Seattle Mariners had a choice to make. They had the first selection in the 1993 draft of amateur players. They were undecided between Alex, who they knew was destined for greatness, and Darren Dreifort, the pitcher from Wichita State. Dreifort was a few years older and closer to being ready to play in the major leagues. Seattle had been faced with a similar choice when the team had the first draft pick in 1987. That time the Mariners bypassed a pitcher who would have brought an immediate return for a player who had more long-term potential. That player was Ken Griffey Jr., and the Mariners were never sorry that they had made that choice.

Alex, on the other hand, was hoping that the Mariners would not draft him. The team with the next selection was the Los Angeles Dodgers. The Dodgers were a National League team, meaning that they would play several games a year against the Florida Marlins in Miami. Alex wanted the chance to play at least a few games in Miami, in front of his family and friends. (At the time Alex was drafted, there was no inter-league play.)

The night before the draft, Roger Jongewaard, Seattle's vice president for scouting and player development, called Alex to say he was pretty certain the Mariners would pick him. Alex asked if they wouldn't reconsider and take someone else so he could be drafted by the Dodgers. "I'm sorry, Alex. I just can't do that," said Jongewaard. Alex was just too good to pass up. He was quick and powerful, with an arm that Jongewaard called "double plus. Two grades above the major-league average."

On Thursday, June 3, Alex gathered with Westminster teammates and friends at J. D. Arteaga's patio for a party that coincided with the draft. In the early afternoon, the call came that he had been the first player selected, by the Seattle Mariners. If Alex was disappointed, he did what he could to hide it. His face even lit up when he spoke of the chance to someday play on the same team with Ken Griffey Jr.

But Alex still had choices to make. He was scheduled to begin classes at the University of Miami later in the summer and would have nearly three months to decide whether to sign with the Seattle Mariners or go to college and play for the Miami Hurricanes.

First, though, Alex had a chance to try out for the United States National team. Team USA invited 19 players, mostly freshmen and sophomores in college, to try out. Alex was the first high school player ever to get an invitation. Alex didn't make the team, but not because of a lack of talent.

Alex didn't want to sign an agreement with a baseball card company that wanted to issue a set of cards on the team. Alex wanted to be free to make deals with other card companies. He didn't get permission to do so and was forced to leave the team as a result.

Alex instead ended up on the U. S. Junior National Squad. He had four hits in two games in the U. S. Olympic Festival in San Antonio in July 1993. In a strange accident, however, he was struck by a wild throw. The ball hit him just below the right eye while he was sitting in the dugout. Alex suffered a broken cheekbone and had to undergo surgery, which ended his summer of baseball.

He turned his attention back to where he would be playing baseball next. Alex had consulted an adviser, Scott Boras, who was handling his contract talks with the Mariners. The negotiations were not going well. For the Mariners to keep the rights to Alex, they would have to sign him before he attended a college class. After that, Alex would return to the draft pool and would be eligible to be drafted by another team in 1994.

It looked like that would be the case, and Alex prepared to start classes at the University of Miami. He planned on majoring in communications, with the ambition of becoming a sportscaster. He also thought about trying out for the Hurricanes' football team. On August 30, however, only hours before his first class at Miami, Alex signed a three-year contract with the Mariners.

Alex was happy with the outcome. "I want to be in the big leagues as soon as possible," he said. A few days after he signed, the Mariners brought him to Seattle and gave him a tour of the city. The highlight of the trip for Alex was a dinner invitation from Ken Griffey Jr. Alex and Griffey hit it off right away.

Ken Griffey Jr.

They spent the evening playing video games and forming the beginning of a close relationship.

Alex wouldn't be teammates with Griffey in the major leagues right away however. He needed some seasoning in the lower levels first. It was too late for Alex to play in the minor leagues in 1993, but he was able to join the Arizona Instructional League, which gave young prospects like Alex a chance to develop. He didn't dominate the league, but the Mariners didn't want him to. They merely wanted him to begin the shift into pro ball and start down the path that would eventually take him to the majors.

After the Instructional League ended, Alex worked out over the winter in Miami. He spent five hours a day running, lifting weights, and fielding grounders. He went to spring training with the Mariners in 1994 and was then assigned to the Appleton Foxes, the Mariners' Class A team in the Midwest League. (Major league teams have "farm systems," consisting of minor league teams, to develop their young players. Class AAA is the highest level in the minors. Class A is the lowest.)

Alex quickly demonstrated that he was too good to stay long at the Class A level. During a 16-game span from late April to mid-May, he hit .406 with 11 homers and 31 RBIs. He was selected to play in the Midwest League All-Star Game in June but was no longer around to take part. A few days earlier, Alex had been promoted to Jacksonville in the Class AA Southern League. Once again, his stay was short. He homered in his first **at bat** with Jacksonville and then continued to hit well. Only three weeks after Alex arrived, he received another promotion.

This one was the big one. This time Alex would move all the way up to the major leagues. On July 8, 1994—at the age of 18 years, 11 months, 11 days— Alex played in his first major league game, against the Boston Red Sox at Fenway Park in Boston.

Alex discussed the game at Fenway Park with one of his coaches (above). Alex (opposite page) wore a face of concentration.

Alex's mother was in the stands at Fenway Park when he made his debut. "It was incredible," she said. "I kept asking myself, 'Am I dreaming?' Alex is a very, very good son."

Alex didn't get any hits in his first game, but he did play well in the field. He handled all his chances at shortstop, including one that required a backhanded stop and long throw from the outfield grass. The next day, in addition to getting two hits at the plate, he made an even more spectacular play. In this one, he dived toward third and snared a hard smash headed for the outfield. He quickly righted himself and nailed the runner with a strong throw to first base.

Seattle fans were eager to see the new sensation. Seattle returned home on Thursday, July 14, for a game against the New York Yankees. Alex was in the lineup and didn't wait long to give the fans a thrill.

Alex put forth his best effort at shortstop in July 1994.

The Yankees' first batter, Bernie Williams, hit a hard ground ball up the middle. Alex dived to his left to snag the grounder, scrambled to his feet, and fired to first to nab Williams.

Alex finished the season back in the minor leagues, where managers thought he could get in playing time without the pressure. He played with the Calgary Cannons in the Class AAA Pacific Coast League. The move turned out to be a good move for Alex and for the organization. In mid-August, major league players went on strike, wiping out the rest of the season. Had Alex still been on the major league squad, he would have had to join the walkout. Instead, he was able to continue playing and hit .311 with 6 homers and 21 RBIs in 32 games with the Cannons.

Alex wasn't done with baseball for the year, though. He went to the Dominican Republic to play baseball in the country's winter league. The trip was a home-coming for Alex, marking his first time back there since his family left for the United States when he was eight. But he had more on his mind. "My mission is to come and learn and try to perfect my game," he said. "I've received some very good reports that Dominican baseball is the strongest in the Caribbean. I'm going to really use this opportunity so that I can establish myself in the majors."

Alex found out just how good the baseball is in the Caribbean winter leagues. He was overmatched but felt like he became a better player because of it. "It was the toughest experience of my life," he said. "I just got my tail kicked and learned how hard this game can be.

"It was brutal, but I recommend it to every young player," Alex added.

5

Breaking Out

In 1995, the Mariners were hoping to win the title in the American League Western Division for the first time in their history, but with a little more than a month to play, their chances didn't look good. The team had endured a lot of injuries, including a broken wrist that caused Ken Griffey Jr. to miss nearly half the year. They trailed the first-place California (now Anaheim) Angels by 12½ games on August 20. After that the Mariners took off, playing great baseball and ending up in a tie with the Angels for first place as the regular season ended. The two teams played a game to break the tie. Seattle won to advance to the playoffs.

The Mariners had a lot of stars. In addition to Griffey, the lineup featured fine hitters like Edgar Martinez and Jay Buhner. The pitching rotation was led by Randy Johnson, a tall lefthander known as the

Big Unit. With a blazing fastball, Johnson was the best pitcher in the American League in 1995.

Alex was sometimes a part of Seattle's great year and sometimes he wasn't. Alex split his season between the Mariners and the team's Class AAA farm team. Following the 1994 season, the Mariners had moved their top farm team to Tacoma, Washington, which was only a few miles south of Seattle. Although getting from one city to the other was easy, Alex didn't enjoy being shipped back and forth. He would rather have stayed in one place, especially if that place were Seattle.

Ken Griffey Jr. was able to help Alex handle some of the ups and downs. Griffey had gone through many of the same things Alex was experiencing. They both found themselves in the major leagues as teenagers, and great things were expected from both, right from the start. Griffey took Alex under his wing, helping him through the challenges he faced. "There's nothing that can happen to him that I haven't already done," said Griffey. "I've been there. He knows if he has a question about anything, all he has to do is ask." Because of the close relationship between Alex and Ken Griffey Jr., Alex got the nickname "Junior Jr."

That was just one of several nicknames. Another, a play on his name, is A-Rod. But his mentor, Griffey, came up with a special name of his own for Alex—Young Buck. Griffey is pleased with Alex's success.

Alex and Ken Griffey Jr. await their turns at bat.

Alex has enjoyed a lot of popularity already, but Griffey good-naturedly keeps the young star in his place. Alex has gotten a lot of ribbing from Griffey, who had received the same treatment when he was the young newcomer.

Alex doesn't mind. He said of Griffey, "He teaches you that you can have fun, respect the game, and also play it hard. When you have that combination, you're going to put yourself in a position to be successful."

But in 1995, the Mariners weren't sure if Alex was ready to stick in the major leagues. They thought he might need another season in the minors. During the course of the year, however, the Mariners needed Alex to fill in when their other infielders were injured.

Alex started the season in Tacoma. But in early May, when Felix Fermin was injured, Alex came up to the Mariners. He started 10 games in Fermin's absence and hit well. He was sent back to Tacoma, though, when Fermin returned at the end of May. A few weeks later, second baseman Luis Sojo was hurt, and Fermin had to play second base. Once again, Alex was called up to fill in at shortstop.

The shuttle continued. Alex came back up in July and started 16 games at shortstop before being sent back to Tacoma in mid-August. He was recalled for the final time at the end of August, and he finally remained with the Mariners for good.

During the time he had played for Tacoma, he was spectacular. He had a .360 batting average with 15 home runs and 45 RBIs in 54 games. He was named the "Most Exciting Player" in the Pacific Coast League and was rated as having the best infield arm in the league. But, of course, Alex liked it better when he was in Seattle, playing for the Mariners.

Each time he was sent back to the minors, he found it harder to make that trip to Tacoma. "Every time I came up [to the majors], I felt it was going to be the last time," he said later. "But I look back on it now, and I'm thankful for the opportunity. I'm a positive person, and I don't look at the demotions. I look at the promotions. If I wasn't doing it right, they wouldn't have kept calling me back up."

Alex played little during the playoffs, but it was still exciting for him. "Just to be on that playoff roster meant so much to me," he said.

The Mariners beat the New York Yankees in their opening playoff series. Seattle trailed in the final game, when Alex entered as a **pinch runner** in the eighth inning and ended up scoring the tying run. The game went into extra innings, and New York took the lead again in the top of the 11th. But the Mariners won in the bottom of the inning as Edgar Martinez doubled home two runs. Ken Griffey raced all the way from first to score the winning run. Alex, who would have been the next hitter, had tears in his eyes as he signaled Griffey to slide. When he saw Griffey was safe, he jumped on his teammate to begin a wild celebration.

Seattle lost the next playoff series, to the Cleveland Indians, and missed out on a chance to advance to the World Series. A memorable scene emerged from the disappointment felt by the Mariners after their loss. Television cameras showed the Mariners' Joey Cora crying on the bench and being consoled by Alex. "I think that little picture itself kind of summed up the whole year, the ups and downs," said Alex. "Joey was crying for everybody—that was everybody's tears in the whole city of Seattle and the state."

Cora and Alex had become close. Cora had taken over as the team's second baseman and would have to work well with whomever the Mariners used at short-stop. Both hoped that shortstop would be Alex, and they worked hard in the spring of 1996 to see that this would happen.

The two came out early each morning during spring training, taking ground balls and flipping them to one another, perfecting the graceful techniques they would need to be a great double-play combina-tion. "Joey's easy to work with, and we'll be good in the field," Alex said. "He calls to me in Spanish [Cora is from Caguas, Puerto Rico]. I call in English. But I answer him back in Spanish, and sometimes he gets on me for my grammar. We're working on that, too."

Alex backs up Joey Cora, who fields the ball from
second base and throws to first.

Alex connects with the ball.

The Mariners at first weren't sure if Alex could play consistently at the major league level, but Alex was. During spring training, he walked into manager Lou Piniella's office and said, "I'm ready."

"I know you are," Piniella replied.

Others weren't so sure, and some members of the media predicted that Alex would struggle. One article reported that he would hit only .250. Alex clipped the article for inspiration to do better.

Alex got off to a good start, as did the Mariners. Seattle moved into first place with an eight-game winning streak in April. In the final game of that streak, Alex hit his first grand slam—scoring four runs—in the majors. A few days later, though, Alex left a game after pulling a hamstring muscle. The injury was enough to put him on the disabled list.

One day after he returned to the lineup in May, Piniella shifted Alex's spot in the batting order. Alex had been hitting eighth, near the bottom of the order. Piniella moved him into the number-two spot. Alex was good at getting on base, either by a hit or a walk, and Piniella wanted more runners on base with the big guns—Griffey, Martinez, and Buhner—coming up to bat.

Hitting ahead of these sluggers also meant that Alex would be seeing better pitches to hit. Pitchers didn't want to risk walking Alex with such great hitters following him.

The shift in the batting order worked well. Over the rest of the season, Alex had a batting average of .367. He also displayed great power. He had his first career two-homer game a few days after his return to the lineup. A few days later he hit his second grand slam of the season and had six RBIs in the game.

I ♥ Alex signs began appearing in the Kingdome, the Mariners' home stadium. On a team filled with exciting and likeable players, Alex was becoming one of the fans' favorites.

Alex was also being recognized outside Seattle. Cal Ripken of the Baltimore Orioles had been voted by baseball fans to be the American League's starting shortstop in the All-Star Game. In early July, Alex was named to the team as a backup to Ripken. He was one of the youngest players ever picked for an All-Star team. Baltimore Orioles manager John Oates noticed that Alex had picked up on many of his hero's habits. "I watch him play now, and he does a lot of things Ripken does before a ballgame to get ready to play," said Oates.

Alex kept up his hot hitting after the All-Star break and ended up on the cover of *Sports Illustrated*, a tremendous honor for a player who was still a few weeks shy of his 21st birthday. One writer said, "Rodriguez plays the position [shortstop] as if he studied his whole life for it." Watching hundreds of games with a critical eye, and learning the habits of different players, had paid off. Alex said, "When I got to the big leagues, no one had to tell me that Cal Ripken was a pull hitter or what Darryl Strawberry did with two strikes."

He started August among the league leaders in many categories, even though he had missed 15 games because of injury. And then he really took off. Twice he was named the American League's Player of the Week and ended up as the league's Player of the Month. Over 29 games in August, he hit .435 with 9 home runs, 30 runs scored, and 28 runs batted in.

Alex appreciates his fans' enthusiasm and always makes time to sign autographs for them.

Alex and Yankee shortstop Derek Jeter are good friends.

One of his homers was a monster shot into the center-field bleachers at Yankee Stadium in New York. After the game that night, Alex and Yankee shortstop Derek Jeter went out to dinner.

The two were still great friends, even though they had to play against one another. They would stay overnight at one another's places when the teams played in Seattle or New York. "I'm Alex's greatest fan," says Jeter. "I brag on him so much that my teammates are sick of me talking about him."

Alex's great performance, along with those of Griffey and the others, helped the Mariners get back into the race for the Western Division title. In the end, though, they fell short and missed the playoffs. Alex had done all he could, however. He finished the season with a batting average of .358. Not only was it the best in the American League, it was the best average by a right-handed hitter in the American League since 1939. He was also the first shortstop to lead the league in batting average since Lou Boudreau of the Cleveland Indians had done it in 1944.

But there was more to his great season than batting average. Alex also was tops in the American League with 3 grand slams, 141 runs scored, and 54 doubles. In addition, he was among the league leaders with 123 RBIs and 36 home runs.

These were outstanding totals for any player, but they were especially great for someone who plays shortstop, a position where fielding is often valued above hitting. Many observers thought that Alex would be named the American League's Most Valuable Player (MVP).

That honor ultimately went to Juan Gonzalez of the Texas Rangers. Alex was a close second. While Alex didn't get the MVP award, he was voted by his fellow players as the Player of the Year for both leagues. He was the youngest player ever to receive this award.

Alex was pleased with the recognition he was getting. But he felt bad that his team didn't make the playoffs. Individual honors are nice, but Alex felt that team success was even more important. He was determined to help the Mariners win even more games in 1997. "Winning and playing hard," he says. "That's what turns me on."

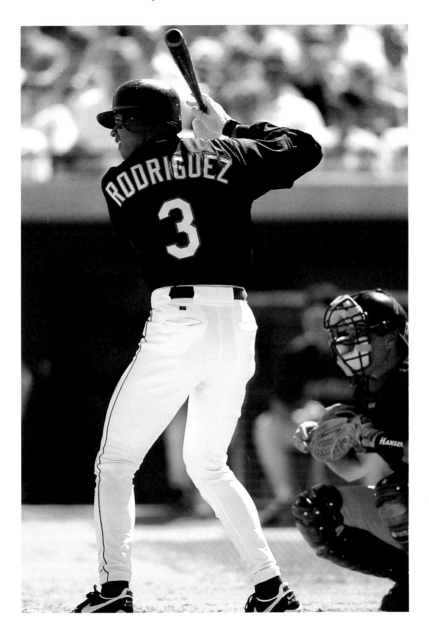

6
A Class Act

Alex continued arriving early to workouts with Joey Cora during spring training in 1997. "I feel like I'm back in high school [having to get up early]," he says. "But at the same time, the rewards are so great, it's all worth it." Alex added that it takes nearly two weeks of fielding and throwing 100 to 200 ground balls per day to get his rhythm back in the infield.

Alex is a tall shortstop, like one of his idols, Cal Ripken of the Baltimore Orioles. Ripken was among the first to break the mold of small shortstops who were good with the glove but not much of a threat with the bat. Alex has followed in that tradition. He's 6 feet, 3 inches tall and weighs close to 200 pounds. Like Ripken, he performs well both in the field and at the plate.

When the regular season opened in 1997, the spot-light was on Alex's teammate and friend, Ken Griffey

Jr., who was hitting home runs at a record pace. Alex was doing well. With the exception of the time he hit for the cycle in early June, he wasn't attracting much attention. That was fine with him, especially since the team was doing well.

The Mariners took off in June, opening up a first-place lead in the Western Division. Alex missed a part of this stretch when he was placed on the disabled list after being injured in a collision at home plate. Alex missed 14 games but came back strong, hitting a home run in his first at bat upon his return to the lineup.

That summer Alex was elected by the fans to be the starting shortstop for the American League in the All-Star Game. He singled his first time up in the game. He got the hit off Greg Maddux, one of the greatest pitchers ever.

In the first Mariners game after the All-Star Game, Alex had four hits in a 12–9 win over the Texas Rangers. The Mariners were now in first place, 4½ games ahead of the Anaheim Angels. But the **pennant** race was far from over.

Anaheim moved into first place in early August, and the two teams battled for the top spot throughout the month. Once again in September, Seattle began to pull away. This time it was for good.

Seattle went on to finish the regular season with a record of 90 wins and 72 losses, 6 games ahead of the second-place Angels. The year had been full of great individual and team performances. The Mariners set a major league record for the most home runs by a team in a season. Ken Griffey didn't break the record for most home runs by a player, but he had hit 56 home runs, the most by an American League player in more than 35 years.

Alex finished the season with a .300 batting average and 23 home runs. The 1997 season hadn't been as outstanding for him as 1996, but it was still good.

Alex forces out the runner on second and sends the ball to first base for a double play.

Most important for Alex and his teammates, though, was that the Mariners had won the American League West title and would advance to the playoffs. It was the second time in three years that the Mariners had done this.

Alex had done little more than watch during the 1995 playoff run. This time, he'd be doing much more. But unfortunately for Seattle, the team's post-season experience was short lived. The Mariners were eliminated, three games to one, by the Baltimore Orioles in the opening playoff round.

Alex hit .313 with a home run but that hadn't been enough. Even though Seattle had made the playoffs, the finish had been disappointing for the Mariners and their fans. But there was still hope for the future. The Mariners were a team with young stars who would continue to generate great excitement.

Alex would be among the leaders of the Seattle Mariners. He and Griffey might compete for the biggest headlines, but there would be more than enough cheers for both of them.

Alex's popularity with the fans isn't just a result of his play on the field. Alex is regarded as one of the nicest players in the game and a true role model. Such success might swell the head of some players, especially a young one. But Alex remains as humble as ever, never forgetting where he has been and how he got to where he is. "For me, the main thing is to be a professional both on and off the field," he explains.

Alex is devoted to his mother. Until 1996 he lived with her in Miami in the off-season, sharing his own bedroom with his German Shepherd, Ripper. He'd play golf in the morning, basketball in the afternoon, and Nintendo at night before bedtime.

Even when he did buy his own house in the Miami area, he wasn't far from his mom. During the season, Alex phones home nearly every day to talk to his mother. "My mom is the whole story of my life," he says. "She's my whole inspiration. If there were hard times [while growing up], I wasn't aware of them. She's done so much for me."

Even though Alex didn't attend college, he understands the importance of reading and getting a good education. He often talks to students in the Seattle area, encouraging them to read. During the 1996 season Alex announced his Grand Slam for Kids educational program to encourage grade school children to work hard on reading, math, physical fitness, and good citizenship. He visits grade schools and holds assemblies to promote the program.

In addition, Alex spends a lot of time working with young people at Boys and Girls Clubs in Miami and around the Seattle area. He remembers what an influence the Boys Club had on him as a youngster growing up without a father around.

Alex held a baseball clinic for young players in the Seattle Kingdome in 1997.

One Boys and Girls Club fund-raising event brought together a bunch of former Miami-area high school ball players. Alex Fernandez, who returned to Miami as a member of the Florida Marlins in 1997, Alex Gonzalez of the Toronto Blue Jays, Alex Ochoa of the New York Mets, and Alex Rodriguez of the Mariners were all there. "Every time a kid said 'Hey, Alex!' all four of us looked around," Gonzalez said.

Alex is an avid reader, especially of motivational books. When the Mariners are on the road, Alex spends some of his time roaming through college campuses and browsing in bookstores. He credits books with helping him develop the right mental attitude to perform at his best and get the most out of his ability. One of his favorite books is *The Winner Within*, written by basketball coach Pat Riley. He always keeps in mind a quote of Riley's he read: "Hard work doesn't guarantee success, but, without it, you don't have a chance."

Alex has had many chances and has made the most of them because of his hard work. And he knows he must continue along the path that has taken him to where he is. Already he has seen others who have strayed from that path. "How many guys haven't I seen come up through the big leagues that are this and that and are big superstars, and two or three years on the road, you don't know who they are?" he says. "So I don't really get overwhelmed by anything. I just try to take it one day at a time. And I know I'm going to be all right."

Career Highlights

Minor Leagues

			G	AB	R	H	2B	3B	HR	RBI	BB	AVG.
1994	Class A	Appleton	65	248	49	79	17	6	14	55	24	.319
1994	Class AA	Jacksonville	17	59	7	17	4	1	1	8	10	.288
1994	Class AAA	Calgary	32	119	22	37	7	4	6	21	8	.311
1995	Class AAA	Tacoma	54	214	37	77	12	3	15	45	18	.360
1996	Class AAA	Tacoma	2	5	0	1	0	0	0	0	2	.200
	Totals		170	645	115	211	40	14	36	129	62	.327

Major Leagues

		G	AB	R	H	2B	3B	HR	RBI	BB	AVG.
1994	Mariners	17	54	4	11	0	0	0	2	3	.204
1995	Mariners	48	142	15	33	6	2	5	19	6	.232
1996	Mariners	146	601	141	215	54	1	36	123	59	.358
1997	Mariners	141	587	100	176	40	3	23	84	41	.300
	Totals	352	1384	260	435	100	6	64	228	109	.314

• Named by *The Sporting News* as Major League Player of the Year, 1996
• American League All-Star Team, 1996, 1997

Glossary

at bat: An official attempt to hit a pitched ball. Hitting a sacrifice, being walked, or being hit by a pitch don't count as an at bat.

batting average: The number of hits a batter gets, divided by the batter's official at bats, carried to three decimal places. For example, if Alex gets 3 hits in 9 at bats, his batting average is .333.

error: A mistake by a fielder that results in a batter or baserunner reaching a base safely.

pennant: The American League championship and the National League championship in Major League Baseball. At the end of the season, the team on top of each of the two divisions within each league plays the other division leader for the league's pennant, or championship. The league champions then go on to play one another in the World Series.

pinch runner: A player who runs the bases for another player.

run batted in (RBI): A run that is scored as a result of a batter getting a hit or, if the bases are loaded, the batter drawing a walk.

scholarship: A sum of money or free tuition granted to a student. Scholarships are awarded on the basis of academic achievements, athletic abilities, or financial need.

Sources

Information for this book was obtained from the following sources: Interview with Alex Rodriguez; Mel Antonen (*Baseball Digest*, October 1996); Rod Beaton (*USA Today Baseball Weekly*, 23 February 1994); Gerry Callahan (*Sports Illustrated*, 8 July 1996, 7 October 1996); Florangela Davila (*Seattle Times*, 23 March 1997); Bob Finnigan (*Seattle Times*, 1 January 1995, 22 February 1996, 18 August 1996, 19 August 1996, 26 September 1996, 22 January 1997, 19 February 1997, 13 March 1997); Bob Kuenster (*Baseball Digest*, January 1997); Tim Kurkjian (*Sports Illustrated*, 14 June 1993, 19 August 1996); Rick Lawes (*USA Today Baseball Weekly*, 5 May 1993, 2 June 1993); Rick Lawes and Marlene Lozado (*USA Today Baseball Weekly*, 9 June 1993); Wayne Lockwood (*Baseball Digest*, July 1997); Candace Oehler (*Mariners' Magazine*, vol 7, issue 2); Rob Rains (*The Sporting News*, 14 October 1996); Selena Roberts (*New York Times*, 18 August 1996); Alan Schwarz (*Baseball America*, 8 July 1996); Bob Sherwin (*Seattle Times*, 28 July 1996, 18 August 1996, 8 October 1996); Claire Smith (*New York Times*, 10 July 1996); Larry Stone (*Seattle Times*, 9 March 1997, 6 May 1997); Jim Street (*Seattle Post-Intelligencer*, 6 August 1996, 14 November 1996, 28 February 1997); George Vass (*Baseball Digest*, February 1997); Laura Vecsey (*Seattle Post-Intelligencer*, 4 April 1996, 5 September 1996); Tom Verducci (*Sports Illustrated*, 18 July 1994, 24 February 1997); Susan Wade (*Baseball America*, 6 January 1997); Kelly Whiteside (*Sports Illustrated*, 22 March 1993); Pete Williams (*USA Today Baseball Weekly*, 28 August 1996, 2 April 1997); Bud Withers (*Seattle Post-Intelligencer*, 4 June 1993, 6 June 1994).

Index

Write to Alex:

You can send mail to Alex at the address on the right. If you write a letter, don't get your hopes up too high. Alex and other athletes get lots of letters every day, and they aren't always able to answer them all.

Alex Rodriguez
c/o The Seattle Mariners
P.O. Box 4100
Seattle, Washington 98104

Acknowledgments

Photographs are reproduced with the permission of: pp. 1, 36, © ALLSPORT USA/Jim Commentucci; pp. 2, 9, 10, 45, © Sports-Chrome East/West, Rob Tringali Jr.; pp. 6, 55, © Mickey Pfleger/Sports California; pp. 11, 52, 59, © ALLSPORT USA/Jed Jacobsohn; pp. 12, 25, 26, © Tom DiPace; pp. 15, 32, © Sports-Chrome East/West, Rich Kane; pp. 18, 21, 22, Seth Poppel Yearbook Archives; p. 28, © SportsChrome East/West, Mike Zito; p. 34, © SportsChrome East/West, Vincent Manniello; p. 35, © ALLSPORT USA/Damian Strohmeyer; pp. 38, 46, © ALLSPORT USA/Otto Greule; pp. 41, 50, © John Klein; pp. 49, 58, © Ben Van Houten.

Front cover photograph by: © SportsChrome East/West, Rob Tringali Jr. Back cover photograph by: © John Klein. Artwork by: Steve Schweitzer.

About the Author

Stew Thornley is the author of several award-winning books on sports history. He has also written several biographies for young readers, *Deion Sanders: Prime Time Player, Cal Ripken, Jr.: Oriole Ironman, Emmitt Smith: Relentless Rusher,* and *Frank Thomas: Baseball's Big Hurt.* A former sportscaster at radio stations in Missouri and central Minnesota, Thornley resides in Roseville, MN.